Learn to
Think Creatively

Mukund Moorthy

Learn to Think Creatively
© *New Horizon Media*

First Edition: July 2009
64 Pages
Printed in India.

ISBN 978-81-8493-325-3
Pro-ya-en-61

Prodigy Books
177/103, First Floor, Ambal's Building
Lloyds Road, Royapettah, Chennai 600 014.
Ph: +91-44-4200-9603
Email: support@nhm.in
Website: www.nhm.in

Prodigy Books is an imprint of New Horizon Media Pvt. Ltd.

The World Health Organization has defined life skills as, 'the abilities for adaptive and positive behaviour that enable individuals to deal effectively with the demands and challenges of everyday life.'

Life skills are essentially those abilities that help promote mental well-being and competence in young people as they face the realities of life. With life skills, one is able to explore alternatives, and understand one's strengths and weaknesses.

Creative Thinking is one of the ten core life skill strategies and techniques listed by WHO (World Health Organisation)

List of core life skill strategies and techniques listed by WHO

Effective communication

Creative thinking

Decision-making

Problem solving

Critical thinking

Interpersonal relationship skills

Self-awareness

Empathy

Coping with emotions

Coping with stress

Content

A different view of the world

Every year in the middle of summer in June, the All England Lawn Tennis and Croquet Club in London plays host to the Wimbledon Championships.

Wimbledon is the oldest tennis tournament in the world. It is also regarded as the most prestigious tournament by the players. Every aspiring tennis professional dreams that one day he will grow up and win the Wimbledon.

The entire tournament lasts for 2 whole weeks. At the end of two weeks of intense competition, a Singles champion is crowned in both the Gentlemen's division and the Ladies' division. A total of 128 players feature in each singles event.

If I were to ask you to determine how many games have to be played in the Ladies division before a champion is crowned, how would you go about calculating the answer?

You would immediately pull out a piece of paper and calculate the following:

128 players means 64 games in the first round, 32 games in the second round, 16 in the third round, 8 in the fourth round, 4 games in the quarter-final, 2 games in the semi-final and eventually the finals of the tournament. That would mean, a total of $64 + 32 + 16 + 8 + 4 + 2 + 1 = 127$ games would be played.

Pat yourself on the back. You are the best. You successfully determined the correct answer. You are a very smart kid to be able to do the necessary math to calculate the answer.

What if I told you that you can arrive at the same answer without having to do any of this complicated arithmetic? Furthermore I will guarantee you that the alternate method that I am going to show you will also be quicker.

We know that there are 128 players in the tournament. There is only 1 champion. That means that every one else in the tournament has to lose. All said there will be 127 losers in the Ladies Singles division. Since each player only loses once, a total of 127 games would be played.

Think about this second solution for a minute. Was this method quicker? Did this method require less calculation? The answer is a big YES.

The first method of arriving at a solution uses conventional thinking. Conventional thinking is how we are taught to think in schools. We are taught that 7 + 2 is 9. We are taught that "impossible" is spelt i-m-p-o-s-s-i-b-l-e. We are taught that the sun rises in the east and sets in the west. These are very important things that we must learn. Nothing wrong about that!

We are educated on understanding problem solving techniques. We are taught to look at questions and recognize what the answers for those questions would be. Examinations test us on how well we remember the answers to these questions. If we do well on these examinations, we are recognized as a "Top Ranker". While it is true that displaying these characteristics makes us a smart and intelligent person, it does not guarantee that we are thinking efficiently. As the Wimbledon example showed, other methods exist that are quicker and simpler.

The second method uses creative thinking. Creative thinking is an alternate way of thinking. In creative thinking, we do not make assumptions. Instead we bend the rules of what has been taught to us – not just to think along a known path but in several different directions.

Creativity is the willingness to explore to play with the ideas and possibilities that might exist along these multiple paths before deciding on the solution. Creative thinking is the ability to invent new and innovative approaches to known problems by combining, changing or re-applying existing ideas. Most often than not, a creative solution is creative because it is a simple, good practical solution that we never thought of before.

Creative thinking does not associate questions with answers. Your Chemistry teacher in school can spend an entire week and make you and everyone else in your class memorize the Periodic table. You might remember it for the rest of the year or if you are really smart, maybe for the next several years. But no teacher can teach you the secrets of creative thinking even if you spend the entire year attending classes. This is not because the teachers are not proficient. This is because creative thinking cannot be taught.

Teachers and parents can provide guidance and opportunities to add creativity to the problems you solve today but cannot make you always use creative thinking in solving problems. Creative thinking becomes an integral part of our thinking process when we incorporate it in our lives. The more we practice the art of thinking creatively, the more predominant it becomes in our brain as a means of thought when we attempt to solve problems.

If solving problems using creative thinking is so much easier and quicker than conventional thinking, why then do we not use it more often?

The answer to this question lies in how our brain is structured and how our brain reacts to various experiences in our lives. The human brain is a complex super computer. It processes information and stores the results for everything that we do both on a conscious level and at the subconscious level. Because we are trained to think in the conventional manner, our brain prefers that approach as the first step to solving any problem. Frequent use of the creative thinking approach breaks that pattern and forces the human brain to incorporate those experiences in solving problems in the future.

The human brain consists of 2 parts – the left side and the right side. Each of the halves controls various character traits. The left half of the brain solves problems logically and sequentially. This half prefers established pieces of information. As students, our schools and teachers train us to use the left half of the brain. As a natural instinct, our brain uses this approach to solve problems. The right half of the brain is spontaneous. The right half solves problems based on hunches and by looking for patterns. The right half of the brain prefers open-ended questions and handles elusive and uncertain information better.

In our schools, we do not get to exercise the right half of the brain as much as we do our left half. For example, History, Mathematics and Physics are some of the subjects that would train the left half of the brain. Painting, dancing and singing are areas that would test the right half of the brain. Now, try and remember how many hours you spend learning subjects that exercise each half of the brain. Obviously the preference is skewed heavily to the left half of the brain. That is another reason why even our brain as powerful as it is, tends to use the left half first unless we force it use the right half as well. In any normal human being, irrespective of their occupation, one half of the brain will be predominant compared to the other half.

People who use the right half of their brain more often are typically very good at acting, drawing, playing instruments etc. Display of mastery in these areas is typically attributed to creativity. Individuals like A R Rahman, Sivaji Ganesan, Mani Rathnam and MF Hussein would fall into this category.

Individuals who predominantly use the left half of the brain usually excel in areas such as research, analysis, mathematics etc. Individuals like C V Raman, Dr Abdul Kalam, Manmohan Singh and Anand Vishwanathan among others fall in this category. Several of us and our parents also belong in this group.

This is not to say that individuals who use the left half of the brain are not creative. These individuals tend to use their left brain more, than they do their right brain. Similarly, the ones usually regarded as "creative" also tend to use the right half of their brains predominantly when compared to their left half.

Irrespective of what you want to become when you grow up, it is important to use both halves of the brain. Conventional thinking is necessary to recognize known patterns. Creative thinking can help you process these known patterns to arrive at the best answers—some of which might be expected and some of which might be unexpected but welcome. Effective solutions are a balance of both the left and right side of the brain.

If you are someone who already incorporates creativity in your daily activities, you are off to a good start. If you have never attempted to think creatively, don't lose heart. Creativity is not a quality that one is born with. The sooner you start to think away from the common patterns, the sooner you will be innovative and brimming with ideas.

The next time you look at an Apple, pause and take account of what information your brain is processing at that moment:

- Is it telling you to eat the fruit?
- Does it make you wonder if the fruit is rotten and contains a worm?

- Does it remind you that "An Apple a day keeps the Doctor away"?
- Does the RED colour of the apple remind you of other red-coloured objects?

Irrespective of what your brain is thinking, you have now started to use the right side of your brain. This simple exercise of imagining various possibilities from staring at an apple is creative thinking. Once you have started to think with that bent, the possibilities are endless...

Conventional thinking

I am sure that you are a very intelligent kid. In school, when your teacher is going over the lessons for the day, you pay very good attention. You write down everything that the teacher wants you to write down. I bet you are also very regular in completing your homework and submitting them on time. When it is time for examinations, you shine and secure the highest marks possible. You memorize everything that was taught to you in class. You answer all the questions that are asked on the question paper. These are the basic secrets to success in an examination.

Give yourself a pat on the back for being so smart and intelligent. You should be very proud of yourself.

Possessing these qualities is a strength that not many can proclaim. If for some reason you have not been able to achieve these as yet, do not fear. These are qualities that you can hone and sharpen easily. Our educational system helps us practice and test these skills on a regular basis. This method of learning or thinking that is taught in our schools is called "conventional thinking".

Conventional thinking teaches us to recognize information in various forms and identify one answer with this information. For example when we talk about India's struggle for independence, we are taught about the various events that occurred during that time. The Rebellion of 1857, the Jalianwalah Bagh incident, the Civil Disobedience movement and the Quit India Movement are a few of the many events that immediately come to mind. When any of these incidents are mentioned even independent of each other, our conventional thinking quickly reacts and connects the dots to remind us that they were associated with India's struggle for independence from the British. Our mind is thus trained to examine certain input and provide a known output.

As mentioned before, the human brain is a highly evolved super computer. The workings of the human brain cannot be easily explained here in its entirety. But a few key aspects of the workings of the human brain will go a long way with understanding how to think creatively. With education, we train our brains to create patterns and store these patterns. At the appropriate moment, the human brain is also trained to recognize these patterns, search for them in storage and eventually retrieve the original event that resulted in the storage of the patterns.

Conventional thinking emphasizes the skills of analysis – teaching us how to understand requests, follow or create a logical argument, figure out the answer, eliminate the incorrect approaches and narrow down to focus on the correct one. For the most part in our lives, we have to follow these approaches.

Every day after school you come back home and go out to play. You join your friends and play a game of cricket. You have played this game for several years now in the street across from your house. The rules of the game maybe a little different from the game of Cricket that Mahendra Singh Dhoni or Sachin Tendulkar play. But they are rules nonetheless.

If someone were to ask you about the rules to the game of Cricket, your answer would be something like this – "There are 2 teams that play against each other. Each team has 11 players. They take turns batting and bowling. The aim of the batting team is to score runs. The aim of the bowling team is to get wickets." That response would be correct and would be a typical example of conventional thinking.

If one's goal is to answer questions, then conventional thinking is a very powerful tool. But if one wants to devise new ways of thinking and invent new ideas, one must explore the opportunities of creative thinking. To do that effectively, one must also learn to recognize the areas where conventional thinking fails. Learning to think differently or using creative thinking in our day to day activities is a lot like learning a new language.

Do you remember the first time you learnt a new language? Maybe it was Tamil, maybe it was Hindi? Or maybe it was English. Learning the Grammar aspect of the language was tough, was it not? You had to forget what you had learnt earlier from your first language. But not completely as the foundations of the second language are very similar to the first language. They both have a set of alphabet. They both have rules which decide how the alphabets are arranged. Learning to think creatively is also like that – you have to remember the foundations of conventional thinking and use them effectively to invent new ideas and find different solutions to the same old set of problems.

With that understanding, let us look at some of the drawbacks of conventional thinking.

1. The more we use conventional thinking as the only way of thinking, the more established they become as the primary form of thinking that our brain uses. It is extremely difficult to change one's way of thinking once they have become established. This is one reason why even when we grow up, we approach life and the various problems the same way as we approached them when we were kids. For example as young children if we were used to seeing our mothers making coffee with milk and sugar then as grown up adults we always associate coffee as being made only with milk and sugar.

2. Conventional thinking is selective in its approach. We only use the information that we already know to make decisions. For example, when we see a juicy stick of orange ice-cream, our mouth waters and we wonder how cold it would feel if we were to lick the stick and eat the ice-cream slowly for us to enjoy it. We do not consider eating the ice-cream with a fork and a knife!

3. Rightness is what matters most in conventional thinking. If you arrive at the wrong answer, there are no bonus points that are awarded for the way we approached the problem. Take the case of your final examination at school. Providing all the correct answers to the questions ensures that you get the highest marks

in the class. Very often are you rewarded the exact same marks for providing similar set of steps without the correct answer. You have to be right at each step to arrive at the correct final answer.

4. There are bounds to what one can achieve with conventional thinking. The main reason for conventional thinking having bounds is because the goal of this mode of thinking is to arrive at an answer. Rules and guidelines are in place to assist us in arriving at this answer.

Conventional thinking is important in our society. It ensures that we can co-exist with others by obeying the basic ground rules. Conventional thinking is also the foundation for science and mathematics. Science and mathematics are primarily responsible for the various advances in our lives today. But conventional thinking alone is not responsible for our lives being so much more simplified than life 50 years back.

For example, if all the inventors and discoverers of the eighteenth and nineteenth century had employed only conventional thinking in their approaches, continents would not have been discovered and modern gadgets would not have been invented. Imagine a life without computers, television, telephones, buses, cars and aircrafts just to name a few inventions. Imagine a life where countries like India and America were not discovered. We would still be living the life of ancient civilizations in isolation.

What then is the secret ingredient that triggered this revolution that resulted in the life that we live today? The answer is Creative thinking.

Breaking patterns

In the 16th century, Krishnadeva Raya was a king well known for fairness. Tenali Ramakrishna or Tenali Rama as he was popularly known was a member of King Krishnadeva Raya's court. He was a very sharp individual. He was popular for his wit and his ability to solve problems that others could not.

One day 3 young men walked into the court of King Krishnadeva Raya with a very unique problem. Their father had just passed away. He had left behind his family property of 17 horses to be divided among his 3 sons. The father had left detailed instructions on how the horses should be divided among his 3 sons. He had stipulated that the elder son should get half the number of horses. The second son was to get one-third of the total number of horses. Finally the father wanted his youngest son to get one-ninth of the total number of horses.

The sons were confused. Dividing the 17 horses as per their father's instructions was not easy. It would require the division to be 8.5 horses for the first son, 5.10 horses for the second and 1.88 horses for the youngest son. Did their father want them to kill the horses to make the division? He had loved the horses and brought them up with so much care. They decided to take the matter up to the king.

King Krishnadeva Raya asked Tenali Rama to solve this conundrum. Tenali Rama asked the brothers to take him to the 17 horses. Once outside, he asked one of the king's soldiers to go to the royal stables and bring one of the king's horses. He told the brothers that he was adding the king's horse as a bonus. The brothers immediately agreed since they now had one more horse to divide among themselves. King Krishnadeva Raya was also surprised. But he knew Tenali Rama well enough to not ask any questions. He waited for Tenali Rama to solve the puzzle. Now there were 18 horses.

Tenali Rama walked up to the first son and asked him to take his share, that is, half of the total number of horses that were present. The first son walked away with 9 horses and he was happy.

Tenali Rama then asked the second son to take his share of his father's property – one-third of the total number of horses. The second son walked away 6 horses and he too was happy.

Tenali Rama finally asked the third son to come. The third son also walked away with his share, one-ninth of the total number of horses. So, he walked away with 2 horses. As you could guess, he was also extremely happy.

This left, Tenali Rama with 18 – 9 – 6 -2 = 1 horse. He promptly asked the king's soldier to return the horse back to the royal stable.

Everyone present including the king was amazed at how Tenali Rama had solved the problem. So how did he manage to do it? Tenali Rama had incorporated creative thinking along with conventional thinking. He did not ignore conventional thinking, but broke the patterns of conventional thinking to arrive at a solution.

You too can be a Tenali Rama. Conventional thinking comes so naturally to us that we do not even recognize it when we think that way. If we are aware of what conventional thinking is, we can recognize our manner of thinking and consider exceptions to incorporate creative thinking.

Here are some of the unique characteristics of conventional thinking and what deviations from that thinking will entail:

- Every problem has only one solution or one right answer.

- The best answer/solution/method has already been found.

- Creative answers are NOT simple.

Some of these concepts are very basic. When we start using creative thinking, our brain will start to question some of these basic foundations of thinking. We should push back on this resistance from our brain. The resistance from our brain is natural because our brain is used to thinking the way it has been since we were born. Making changes to the way we think and the way we approach problems should be gradual. The more we incorporate this new mode of thinking, the more normal it will seem to our mind. The point with creative thinking is to NOT completely ignore conventional thinking. Doing so will mean you might be ignoring even the basic ground rules. Finding a balance of when to deviate away from conventional thinking and when to return back to it is the most practical and successful solution.

Creativity is the ability to imagine something new. The "new" approach can apply to anything and everything in our lives. We imagine and invent new ideas by combining, changing or reapplying existing ideas. Yes, some of the biggest creative breakthroughs in our lifetime are brilliant and astonishing, but there are many that are just simple, good practical ideas that no one thought of before.

Everyone, you and me included has extensive creative ability. The younger we are, the easier it is for us to use our creative abilities. For young adults who feel that they have not been creative for several years, these tendencies can be re-awakened. What is needed is to make a commitment to creativity and dedicating the time necessary to build the skills.

Creativity is also the ability to accept change and newness – a willingness to play with ideas and possibilities, a flexibility of outlook, the habit of enjoying the good and the easy, while looking for ways to improve it are all that yield the many opportunities.

There is a common misconception that being creative is easy. The popular belief is that it comes very naturally for those who are talented. How convenient would it be if being creative is as easy as flicking your fingers for one single stroke of brilliance? Unfortunately it is usually not. One has to work very hard and has to constantly improve on the ideas and solutions by making gradual alterations and refinements to the current solution. As a creative person, you recognize that irrespective of how developed your current solution is, there is always room for improvement.

Here are tips and tricks to deviate from conventional thinking and incorporate creative thinking into our lives with very little effort:

Problems are your friends

Some times our reaction to a problem is much bigger than the problem itself. We tend to deny that a problem exists until it is too late. In some cases, the difficulty of the problem seems bigger because we did not address it in a timely manner.

I am sure your English teacher at school gives you regular homework. On some days the homework is due the next day. In some cases, the home work is due a week later. When the home work is due a week later, do you still come home and complete the assignment early? No. We wait till the last minute to address any problem, even if it is a homework assignment.

Instead, we should approach a problem as an opportunity. The happiest and successful people welcome and even seek out problems. Meeting problems as challenges are opportunities to improve things. A problem is after all seeing the difference between what you have and what you want. By recognizing and believing that there is something better than the current situation we open the opportunity for a positive action.

By seeking problems to solve, we will become more confident. Confidence in turn will result in seeking unique solutions.

Abolish the word "Cannot"

Having an attitude that a task cannot be done is giving up even before starting. With that attitude one is only wasting time working on the task. People who usually approach tasks with this attitude have a closed mind. As a result we will not be willing to explore any ideas. Some of us use this mechanism to satisfy ourselves when we resist the urge to be creative.

In some cases we also tend to think that the problem can be solved, just not by us. We believe that only an expert will be able to solve the problem. We fail to recognize that we might be that expert. Maybe we do not possess the level of expertise when we approach the problem but we definitely will be an expert after we have solved the problem. History has several examples where a unique concept or idea was developed by someone who has almost zero expertise in that area:

- The Wright brothers who invented the airplane had no expertise in aerodynamics. They were bicycle mechanics.

- Major advances in submarine design were made by an English clergyman G. W. Garrett and an Irish schoolmaster, John P. Holland.

- Automobile giant General Motors invented Freon, the refrigeration chemical.

- The ball point pen was invented by a printer's proof reader, Ladislao Biro and not by a mechanical engineer.

- The pioneers of the photography industry Kodachrome was founded by 2 musicians.

As should be obvious now, a good mind with a positive attitude and some problem solving skills will go far in solving any problem. One should be interested in and committed to the problem. When one is willing to spend the effort necessary and motivated enough to identify a solution, the results are very often extremely encouraging.

Getting Back to Childish Tendencies
Whether we want to acknowledge it or not, we are all creative. The extent of creativity though varies from individual to individual. Our approach to creativity depends on our education and our experiences.

Take the case of a 3 year old child. Say you were to give this child a cup of ice cream, a fork and a spoon. What do you think the child will do with this spoon, fork and ice cream? The child would not be aware of what a spoon or a fork is unless he or she has seen someone use a spoon or fork. The child would probably try using the fork to taste the ice cream before realizing that the spoon is much more convenient to eat the ice cream. Why?

As you ponder the response to the question above, let me ask you another question. What do you think will happen if you were to give the same bowl of ice cream, the fork and the spoon to a grown up adult. I can assure you that the adult would use the spoon to eat the ice cream. The fork would not be touched. This is because adults are trained in the use of the spoon and the fork. On spotting the food to be eaten, ice cream in this case, their brain instructs them to use the spoon to eat the food rather than the fork.

Eating ice cream with a fork is not wrong. Using a spoon is the smart approach. With experience we often miss opportunities to explore solutions. Children on the other hand explore such opportunities. I am not asking you to consider eating ice cream with a fork the next time you are in a restaurant. All I am asking you to do is to consider going back to our childish tendencies to think creatively. The more we think like children, the more we let our minds explore alternate solutions. When we solve problems through the eyes of children we also tend to have more fun. We will be sure to enjoy the process.

Opinion of Others

We live in a society where we are often judged for what we do and how we are perceived by others. Incorporating creative thinking will usually involve going against the norm and as a result not conforming to what is ordinary. We should be prepared to face such situations and not fear them.

From a very young age, we are told to obey rules. We are informed of what is accepted and what is not. When we deviate from what is accepted, we are considered to be wrong and most often we are punished. As long as we are not insulting people or ridiculing people's religious beliefs, we should be open to deviating from what is accepted. Keep in mind that deviating from the accepted is not the same as breaking rules.

Whether you like it or not, people always have an opinion. Whether you know those people or not, they will have an opinion of you. There is really nothing that you can do to stop others from having an opinion about you. Since others are going to talk about you, you might as well relax and let your creativity and individualism flow. Almost every famous contributor to the betterment of civilization was ridiculed and sometimes even jailed.

Consider Galileo. Galileo Galilei was an Italian mathematician and astronomer from the 16th century. Years prior, another astronomer by the name of Copernicus had stated that Earth was at the centre of the solar system. Galileo disagreed with this theory. Galileo stated that the Sun was in fact in the centre of the solar system. He also added that the Earth was one of many planets that revolved around the sun. Galileo's theory was so radical that it angered everyone including the church. To punish him, he was imprisoned at home and eventually spent the rest of his life under house arrest.

Progress is made only by those who are strong enough to endure being laughed at or criticized. Solutions are often new ideas. New ideas being strange are usually greeted with laughter, contempt, or both. That should not discourage us from working on finding a solution.

Fear of Facing Failure

Thomas Alva Edison was a very famous American inventor and scientist. His most famous invention is the electric light bulb or the incandescent lamp. He invented the light bulb after several years of hard work and research. In his search for the perfect filament for the incandescent lamp he tried anything and everything he could think of including the whiskers from his pet cat. In all, he tried about 1800 different materials for his filament. After about 1000 attempts, a fellow scientist asked him if he was frustrated at his lack of success. He replied that to the contrary he was quite proud of his work and the level of success he had achieved. He now had gained enough knowledge to know a thousand things that would not work as a filament for the light bulb.

Fear of failure is one of the major obstacles to creativity and problem solving. The cure is to change our attitudes about failure. Failures in the process of solving a problem should be expected and accepted. Failures are nothing but learning tools. They help focus our path to success. Failing is a sign of action. The sign of action is still one more step we have taken than not trying at all. We should always remember that every failure shows us one idea that did not work like Edison said. When we succeed after several failures, we will enjoy the feeling of accomplishment that comes after a long struggle.

Modern society has for some reason conceived the idea that the only unforgivable thing is to fail or make a mistake. Actually failure is an opportunity. Mistakes show that something is being done. As creative people, we have to realize and accept emotionally that making mistakes is a positive effect. Mistakes are educational and can lead to success because they mean we are doing something and not sitting idle.

Our fear of failure guides our attempts at trying a new task – whether it is learning to play a musical instrument, learning to paint a landscape or attempting to dance. We could only try 3 new tasks in a year because we want nothing but success. At the end of the year, we would have 3 Successes and 0 Failures. Now suppose the following year we ignore the failures and tried anything and everything possible. We might try 100 tasks. We might fail at 70 of those tasks. At the end of that year, our score would be 30 Successes and 70 Failures.

Which would you rather have - 3 successes or 30, ten times as many? And consider the amount of knowledge we would have amassed with what the 70 failures would have taught us!

It is therefore important for us to work on breaking those patterns of conventional thinking.

Mental flexibility

One of the greatest barriers to you being creative is YOU. I am not joking. I am serious. We carry around a lot of thought in our heads. These thoughts interfere with the new thoughts that we have. When our mind is filled with so many different thoughts it leaves no room for any newer ones.

Consider the 5 items that we will see when we wake up. The items are probably tooth paste, tooth brush, towel, soap and shampoo. Our mind has a specific use for each of these objects and puts them to that specific use without much thought. We need to start looking at the world in new ways. When you wake up tomorrow morning and before you use the 5 items listed above, come up with alternate uses for each of those objects. This will trigger your mind to always consider alternate approaches.

Are you familiar with practicing Yoga? Yoga is an ancient form of exercise that allows one to control and unify one's body and mind. The poses that one performs during Yoga are quite complex. A newcomer trying to perform these complex poses will not be able to do them. But after weeks of practice, you are able to twist and turn the body to perform the same complex poses that were impossible weeks back.

Creative thinking requires you to do the same to your mind. To make the mind flexible, one should practice to think differently. There are several other attitudes that are key to one being creative. The more flexible we make our minds to these attitudes the sooner we can come up with creative ideas.

Curiosity

Creative people want to know things – all kinds of things – just to know them. The questions could be in areas that they are already experts in. The questions could be in areas that they have absolutely no knowledge in. This is because wanting to know something does not require a reason. Creative people ask questions because they do not know the answer. It is as simple as that. When we get answers to questions, we increase our knowledge. Knowledge is enjoyable and often useful in strange and unexpected ways. Knowledge and especially wide ranging knowledge is necessary for creativity to flourish at its fullest. The best ideas flow from a well equipped mind.

In addition to knowing, creative people also want to know why. What are the reasons behind decisions, problems, solutions, events and facts? Why do we do certain things in a certain way and not another? Do you know why we drive cars and buses on the right side of the road? Has anyone tried driving automobiles on the left side of the road? You might already know the answers to these questions. If not, you might want to find out. You will not be given the First Rank in your class for knowing the answers to these questions. But you will probably use the knowledge you gain from these answers to solve some other problem.

A curious person asks a question for a positive reason. The idea is not to obstruct progress or offer a negative view in solving the problem. The creative person should also be prepared to understand that for many of the things that we do in our lives, there is no real reason why we do it that way. Therefore, ask questions of everyone. Ask the same question to different people to compare the answers. Look into areas of knowledge you have never before explored – music, entertainment, sports, politics, arts etc.

We also need knowledge gained by study and research. We must then put our knowledge to work by thinking hard and long-drawn-out experimentation. Difficulties and setbacks are natural and every creative genius encounters them. One must plan to persevere through all the setbacks. Planning to persevere is planning to succeed.

Challenge

Curious people like to identify and challenge the assumptions behind ideas, proposals, problems, beliefs and statements. Many assumptions are necessary and solid. But many are assumptions because others have assumed facts unnecessarily. When we break out of these assumptions, we will come up with a new idea, a new path, and a new solution.

For example, when we think of school, we traditionally think of a physical campus with classrooms, a library and some nice trees. But why must school be a place with students and teachers? Thus, the electronic school now exists as online universities. Students go to school sitting right at home. You are probably familiar with a primitive form of this idea — correspondence courses used by students to get their graduate degrees.

When we think of an electric motor, we automatically think of a rotating shaft machine. But why make that assumption? Why can't an electric motor have a linear output, moving in a straight line rather than a circle? With such a challenged assumption came the linear motor with its ability to power electric trains and elevators.

In France, a common brand of fruit juice is sold with a fully grown pear inside each of the bottles. The bottle is narrow necked. So how did the pear get inside the bottle?

The common assumption that one will make is that the pear was fully grown before it was put into the bottle. That is a fair assumption to make. With that assumption in mind, the solutions could be,

A. to close the neck or bottom of the bottle after inserting the fruit, or

B. use a plastic bottle to be able to heat shrink the tubing, or

C. use a wide mouthed bottle

Now what if we do not assume that the fruit was fully grown before it was put into the bottle? We could grow the pear as a bud from inside the bottle. It would take 6-9 months, but it could be done.

Always challenge assumptions as even the most obvious of assumptions can lead to a totally different and sometimes wrong answers.

Constructive discontent

You have probably heard of the term constructive criticism. Constructive discontent is a similar concept. The discontent is not a complaining kind of discontent. This is the ability to see a need for improvement and to propose a method of making that improvement. Constructive discontent is a positive, enthusiastic discontent, reflecting the thought that we recognized a better way to make the current solution better.

Constructive discontent is necessary for a creative problem solver. This is because if we are happy with everything the way it is, we will not want to change anything. Only when we become discontent with something, we see a problem which we want to solve and improve on it.

Another mark of constructive discontent is the enjoyment of challenge. Creative people are eager to test their own limits and the limits of problems. They are willing to work hard, to persevere and not give up easily.

Problems are Opportunities for Improvement

The attitude of constructive discontent searches for problems and possible areas of improvement. But many times problems arrive by themselves. Such unexpected and perhaps unwanted problems are not necessarily bad. They often permit solutions that leave the world better.

For example a couple of hundred years back the first margarine was made from beef fat, milk, water, and chopped cow udder. It wasn't extremely tasty or healthy. In the early 1900s, a shortage of beef fat created a problem.

Beef fat was no longer available to be used as an ingredient. The margarine makers turned to vegetable fats from various plants. Soybean, corn, and sunflower oils they used then are still used to make margarine today. The big difference is that the margarine of today is healthier and tastes better than the margarine of the 1900s.

All Problems can be Solved

Problems are solved by a commitment of time and energy. When this commitment is present, few things are impossible. The belief in the solvability of problems is useful early on in attacking any problem. Many problems at first seem utterly impossible to solve. Some people will even be scared. Those who take on the problem with confidence will be the ones most likely to think through or around the impossibility of the problem.

The first several times we use creative techniques to solve problems, we must completely believe that we will find the solution. Later on, by experience we will know that we will find a way to eliminate or help alleviate almost every problem.

It is important to remember that most people fail because they spend only nine minutes on a problem that requires ten minutes to solve. Using creativity to solve problems is hard work and requires fierce application of time and energy. There is no quick and easy way out.

One should also remember the critical truth in problem solving. The goal is to solve the problem, not to implement a particular solution. When one solution path is not working, we should shift to another. Path fixation can sometimes be a problem for those who do not understand this. They become overcommitted to a path that does not work. This usually results in frustration. There is no commitment to a particular path, only to a particular goal.

Suspension of Judgment and Criticism

Many new ideas are initially new and unfamiliar. The idea might seem strange, odd and sometimes bizarre. Only later do people recognize them to be great. Many ideas as they were originally imagined are probably different. But they lead to practical, beautiful and elegant things. Thus, it is important for the creative thinker to be able to suspend judgment when new ideas are arriving.

A creative thinker should have an optimistic attitude towards ideas in general. One will have to hear phrases like "That will never work", "That is no good" and "That is impossible" several times from others while working on a creative solution. Hospital sterilization and antiseptic procedures, television, radio, the Xerox machine, and stainless steel, all met with criticism and even hostile rejection before the public realized the value of the ideas and how much more convenient it would make human life.

Some of our everyday tools that we now love and use daily were heavily opposed and criticized when they were originally presented:

Aluminum cookware	-	No one wanted them.
Teflon pans	-	There was no market for the product.
Erasers on pencils	-	The public were convinced that erasers only encouraged carelessness.
Computers	-	Thomas Watson, President of IBM said in 1943, "I think there is a world market for maybe 5 computers."

Remember then that an idea may begin to look good only after it becomes a bit more familiar. The idea would then be seen in a slightly different context. Even a very wild idea can serve as a stepping stone to a practical, efficient idea. By too quickly bringing our judgment into play, these fragile early ideas and their source can be destroyed. When we suspend judgment, our idea-generating powers will be free to create without the restraint of fear or criticism.

Creative people are comfortable with imagination and with thinking so-called weird, wild, or unthinkable thoughts, just for the sake of stimulation. During mental playfulness, all kinds of strange thoughts and ideas can be entertained. And the mind will eventually find something useful in it.

Finding Good in the Bad

When faced with poor solutions, people who think creatively do not cast the solutions away. Instead they consider what good might be in the poor solution. This is because there may be something useful even in the worst of ideas. And however little that good may be the power of creative thinking can be used effectively to harness that good or better yet, make it greater. Creative thinking enables us to adapt or incorporate some of these good things into a more acceptable solution, whether derivative of the original or not?

We typically tend to believe that a bad solution is bad through and through, in every aspect. In fact the bad solution may have some good parts we can borrow and use on a good solution. Or by changing something very small on the bad solution, it might be possible to completely transform the solution from poor to excellent. This is because usually any bad solution has just one really glaring bad part. When that one bad part was remedied one was left with a good solution.

A Problem can also be a Solution

A fact that one person describes as a problem can sometimes be a solution for someone else. As you already know a creative thinker can find good ideas in bad solutions. Creative thinkers also look at problems and wonder if there is anything good in the problem.

For example in the 1940s, a new adhesive called as cyanoacrylate or Super Glue was introduced. Super Glue was a very powerful adhesive. It had the power to attach any two pieces together. In fact, the glue was so powerful that the user of the adhesive had to be extremely careful to not get it in touch with bare human skin. Super Glue had the power to glue one's fingers together with it. This was a problem since the skin bond was permanent. But this would turn out to be a solution for one group. In 1966, the power of the cyanoacrylate adhesive was used in the Vietnam War to retard bleeding in wounded soldiers until they could be brought to a hospital.

A few years back, chemists were experimenting with adhesives and accidentally came up with one that was so weak you could peel it right back off. A good glue is often defined by its hold strength and the shear strength. On this newly invented glue the hold strength and the shear strength were way below the minimum standards for the product to be sold to the public. But the scientists saw a solution in the problem. They launched a product called "Post-it Notes" which capitalizes on the ability of the weak glue to allow for pieces of paper to be peeled off.

The power of ideas

Creativity is much more than just creating ideas. But the contrary is not true. New ideas require the use of creativity for them to be considered new. After all, if one were to imagine the same things that we currently use today what additional value do we contribute and why would anyone listen to what we have to say.

The power of ideas comes primarily from Divergent thinking and our imagination skills.

Divergent Thinking

Convergent thinking, occurs when a person gathers facts, evidence or experiences from a variety of sources to solve a problem. The result is one answer that hopefully is correct. In school we all have learned a large amount of knowledge that could be classed as factual. We have often been tested for the correct answers — so in many cases convergent thinking comes natural to us.

An example of convergent thinking would be solving a math problem such as 2+2= 4.

Divergent thinking is a thought process or method used to generate creative ideas by exploring many possible solutions. It is often used in conjunction with convergent thinking, which follows a particular set of logical steps to arrive at one "correct" solution. Divergent thinking typically occurs in a spontaneous, free-flowing manner, where ideas are generated in a random, unorganized fashion. Many possible solutions are explored in a short amount of time, and unexpected connections are drawn. Following divergent thinking, ideas and information are organized and structured using convergent thinking. Divergent thinking occurs when we start with a stimulus and rather than look for one answer instead generate many ideas or possible solutions.

In the following set of questions, there are two responses – one a relatively divergent reply and the other a relatively convergent reply. Let us see if you can identify the type of the response.

1. I would like to improve my education
   - I suggest you sign up for a community college course
   - Well, there are many possibilities, aren't there?

2. Let us discuss the scheduling problem
   - I have already got it solved
   - What are the factors involved?

3. Do you have any money?
   - Yes, but not very much.
   - Why do you want to know?

4. What kinds of products should we be developing?
   - Let us stick to computer related products.
   - To answer that question, we have to think about marketing strategy.

5. I would like to get to know you better
   - Let us talk.
   - What would you like to know?

The divergent response in each of the questions above is Option 2. If you are still confused as to what makes a response convergent as opposed to divergent consider which of the above responses is not a Yes/No response. That one is the divergent response. A divergent response will also allow for the conversation to be continued beyond this initial question.

Developing Our Imagination

We can use our visualization skills to remember the names of people we meet. When you meet a person, take about five seconds and focus your attention on getting his or her name. Make this a deliberate effort—say the name aloud or ask the person to repeat it and make sure that you have heard it and are conscious of it. You might say something like, "I am teaching myself to remember names, so I hope you don't mind if I take a second or so to get your name clearly." The other person will probably find this flattering, which will serve an additional purpose in starting off positively.

As you say the name aloud for the second time, visualize the name written in bold letters across the person's chest. Use letters whose shapes seem to match with his or her personality or appearance. For example, if Archana is a tall person, use a thin and graceful script for her. If Manoj is a plump person, use a heavy and rounded capital letter for him. Later when you want to recall the name, you can assist your regular memory process by re-collecting the letters and "looking up" the person's name in your visual memory.

Give special attention to a positive attitude in recalling people's names. Don't tell yourself "I can never remember names" or you will not remember them. Practice imprinting them carefully in your brain and you will notice improvement in your skill.

All of these techniques have the same purpose. To enrich the associations, increase the emotional content, and diversify the form of the mental image you want to imprint in your brain.

Now you are well on your way to developing ideas. But keep in mind that ideas just don't pop up in your head like mushrooms after a rain. There are several different ways in which ideas occur to individuals. Below are some of the more common methods.

Evolution

This means gradual improvement. New ideas originate from other ideas. New solutions germinate from previous ones. The new solutions will be slightly better than the older ones. Many of the very sophisticated things we enjoy today were developed through a long period of constant improvement. Making something a little better here and a little better there eventually makes it something significantly better — and at times very different from the original itself.

For example, the flat screen televisions of today were not invented out of the blue. Television when it was first invented in the 1930s was a huge heavy box that could only display pictures in Black and White. Over time, colour televisions were introduced and the size of the televisions became smaller while at the same time they also became lighter. A few years back the televisions became digital. And now, televisions are high-definition digital, light and so big that they can replace the big screens that we see in movie theatres. The power of gradual changes through the process of evolution should not be underestimated.

Synthesis

In this method, two or more existing ideas are combined into a third, new idea. It is possible that each of these ideas individually might not be unique in itself. But the combined idea might be something very unique.

For example, listening to music on CDs is a very popular pastime. Similarly, reading books is also a very popular hobby for many individuals. Some very creative individuals in the publishing industry brought both of these ideas together and launched the concept of audio books. In this case, all of the three ideas are very popular today.

Revolution

In some cases, the best new idea is a completely different one, a marked change from the previous one. This will usually be a deviation from the normal.

What is your favourite song from a movie? You probably own an audio cassette or a CD of that movie at home. When you want to listen to the song, you use your cassette player or CD player to play it back. Until a couple of years back, this was the most popular method of owning the song and playing it back at your will.

But now with the introduction of the iPod and other MP3 players, a new revolution has taken over the music industry. Songs are released on CDs but they are stored on one's personal music player. In some cases like the iPod, the songs are purchased over the internet and transferred to your iPod via your computer.

This new idea is a marked and completely different one from the previous idea.

Re-Application

Re-application is to look at something old in a new way. We need to move beyond what these items are identified to serve today. We should remove our previous opinions, prejudices, expectations and assumptions and discover how something can be reapplied. The same object might serve several purposes.

For example, a paperclip can be used as a tiny screwdriver if filed down. Paint can be used as a kind of glue to prevent screws from loosening in machinery. Dishwashing detergents can be used to remove the DNA from bacteria in a lab. General purpose spray cleaners can be used to kill ants and other small pests.

Changing Direction

Many creative breakthroughs occur when attention is shifted from one angle of a problem to another. This is sometimes called creative insight.

Coca-Cola or Coke was a very popular soft drink in the United States since the early 20th century. In 1993 to appeal to the health conscious Americans, the company decided to change the formula of the drink. The revised formula was called as New Coke and launched in the market. Unfortunately several of the Americans loved the original Coke taste and the Coca-Cola Company had to re-launch the original Coke. But in doing so, the company also very slightly revised the formula of New Coke and launched a product called Diet Coke. Today, both Original Coke and Diet Coke are very popular drinks all around the world.

Given that the launch of New Coke was a disaster, every one expected the Coca-Cola Company to withdraw the product from the market. Instead, they shifted the attention of the problem and now have 2 successful products to show for their efforts.

Windows to a creative world

Many people limit their thinking by assuming that thinking skills are genetically fixed and simply fail to challenge themselves. In precisely the same way that your heart, lungs and muscles improve their functioning after a few weeks of jogging and continue to improve with a steady increase in exercise program, your brain skills will also improve over time if you make increasing demands on them.

In school, I am sure that you have an athletic team. The athletic team competes in various track and field competitions. The team does not start practicing a week before the competition, but practice throughout the year.

Practicing throughout the year keeps the muscles sharp and flexible. That way when the athletes need to use them at the competition, their bodies are in the best possible shape.

The brain is just like your knees or your hamstring. To be effective at winning the creativity competition, the brain should be exercised. All the skills — concentration, observation, memory, logical reasoning, forming hypothesis, generating options, making associations, recognizing patterns and making inferences — will respond to exercise. We simply have to decide which skill we want to develop first, give it our attention and put it through an exercise program.

By using a proper approach, we should work out ways to exercise the mind and continue it over a period of weeks or even months. Of course, if we undertake a rigorous and overly disciplined training regimen without enjoying it, we might probably not stick to the exercise regimen long enough to see any improvements.

Skill building involves replacing old habits with newer and more effective ones. Changing our habits serves as a useful starting point. If we can train ourselves to systematically isolate a habit and practice to replace it, we can easily develop any brain skill we choose using the same technique. We just make practice of that skill into a habit and it will come along automatically.

For example, you might have the habit of biting your finger nails. Your parents ask you repeatedly not to bite your finger nails. You want to listen to your parents and you try hard to overcome the problem. But you are unable to do so. Here is an alternate method to try. Every time you feel as though you want to bite your nails, try to clap your hands once and bite your lip instead. It might be very difficult at first. But over time, you will realize that you are not biting your nails as often you used to.

I am sure you are well versed in using the computer. I am also very sure that you are probably much better at using the computer than your parents. But computers also have a problem. Once in a while, the computers do not respond to the input and appear to be stuck or frozen. To overcome the problem, you re-boot the computer. Once the computer is re-booted, everything seems to work much faster and efficiently.

You will need to do the same to solve the exercises given in this book. Perform a re-boot of your brain so you can expunge all earlier misconceptions. When your brain re-boots, make an effort to include all the techniques and ideas we have discussed earlier in this book.

Thinking Exercise One

Write down 10 alternate uses for the following objects:

A. Paper-clip

1. ______________________________

2. ______________________________

3. ______________________________

4. ______________________________

5. ______________________________

6. ______________________________

7. ______________________________

8. ______________________________

9. ______________________________

10. ______________________________

B. Brick

1. ______________________________

2. ______________________________

3. ______________________________

4. ______________________________

5. _______________________________

6. _______________________________

7. _______________________________

8. _______________________________

9. _______________________________

10. ______________________________

C. Ball-point pen

1. _______________________________

2. _______________________________

3. _______________________________

4. _______________________________

5. _______________________________

6. _______________________________

7. _______________________________

8. _______________________________

9. _______________________________

10. ______________________________

Thinking Exercise Two

Combine one word from Column A and one word from Column B. Consider combining words to create a NEW product that people would buy from a store.

Column A	Column B
pencil	run
theater	key
rubber	safety
window	party
ice ceam	button
candy	magazine
book	collect
dog	vacation
blanket	computer
shoes	write
egg	jewelry
television	sing
credit card	exercise
bicycle	leather
cup	play

Thinking Exercise Three

Each of these diagrams portrays a familiar phrase or a figure of speech. The first one in cryptic form stands for "man overboard". Can you identify the other two?

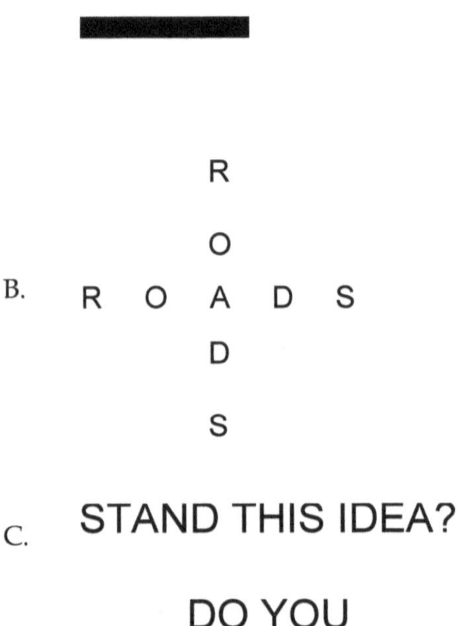

Thinking Exercise Four

A. Can you correct this equation by moving only one matchstick?

B. How many squares can you find in this diagram?

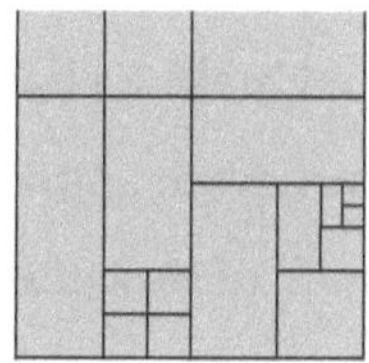

C. How many triangles can you find in this diagram?

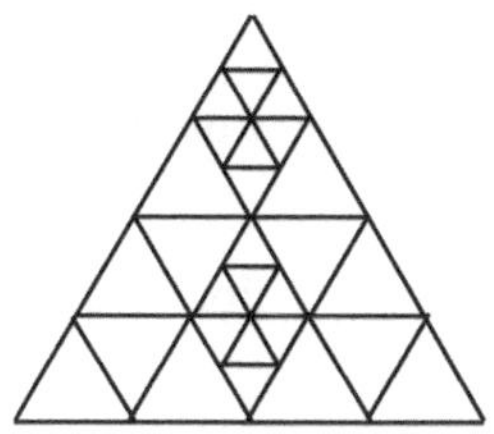

Solution

ONE

This exercise has no wrong answers. Your creativity is what decides the number of responses you were able to come up with for each of the objects. For example, the 10 alternate uses to a paper clip are:

1. Screw driver for narrow/small headed screws.

2. Lock opener in cases of lost keys.

3. Dirt remover/cleaner for narrow spaces.

4. A string of clips can make a chain (jewelry)

5. A string of clips can make a bracelet.

6. Scrubber for removal of wax after a candle has burned down.

7. The edge of a clip can adjust a wick in a glowing lamp.

8. The edge of a clip dipped in ink can be used to write a fine font.

9. A paper clip can be used in an emergency when your shirt button pops off.

10. The edges of a piece of cloth can be kept flat by using a paper clip.

TWO

This exercise has no wrong answers. There are several combinations that you can arrive at. The number of word combinations is only limited by your creative talents.

Let us take the first word from Column A - "**pencil**". We can pick any word from Column B. Let us choose the fifth word - "**button**". How do we combine these two words? We can make a mechanical color pencil with 4 colors – blue, green, red and black. A button will select the color to be used. Now we have combined the two words, "pencil" and "button" to create a brand new idea.

THREE

A. Man Overboard

B. Crossroads

C. Do you understand this idea?

FOUR

A.
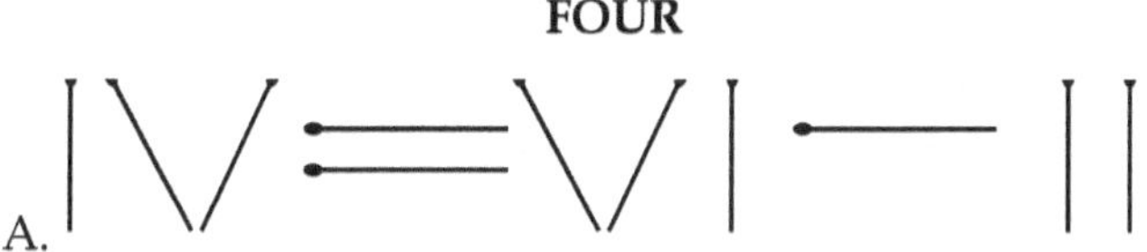

B. 16 squares.

C. 39 triangles.

Prodigy books

Biographies

Abdul Kalam
Charles Darwin
Marie Curie
Visvesvaraya
Srinivasa Ramanujan
Newton
Einstein
James Watt
Sir JC Bose
Alexander Graham Bell
Gandhi
Jawaharlal Nehru
Mother Teresa
Ambedkar
Bhagat Sigh
Tipu Sultan
Rani of Jhansi
Akbar
Shivaji
Bharati
Rabindranath Tagore
Martin Luther King
Alexander the Great
Napoleon
Adolf Hitler
Charlie Chaplin
Walt Disney
Bill Gates

Narayana Murthy
Columbus

Classics Retold

Homer's Iliad
The Odyssey
The Tempest
Hamlet
The Merchant of Venice
Twelfth Night
Romeo and Juliet
Macbeth

Other Titles

The Universe
Hinduism
Global Warming
Abraham Lincoln
The New 7 wonders of the World
Life
Tsunami
Dinosaurs
Ganga
World War II
Madras - Chennai
Exam Tips
Television
Effective Communication
Creative Thinking